The Handmaid's Tale

BY MARGARET ATWOOD

BOOK ANALYSIS

By Georgina Murphy

The Handmaid's Tale

BY MARGARET ATWOOD

Bright
≡Summaries.com

MARGARET ATWOOD

CANADIAN WRITER

- **Born in Ottawa (Canada) in 1939.**
- **Notable works:**
  - *The Circle Game* (1964), poetry collection
  - *Survival: A Thematic Guide to Canadian Literature* (1972), literary criticism
  - *Alias Grace* (1996), historical crime novel

Margaret Atwood is the author of a vast range of both fiction and non-fiction works, including 17 poetry collections and 16 novels. She won the Man Booker Prize in 2000 for her novel *The Blind Assassin* and has been nominated for the award on three further occasions: for *The Handmaid's Tale* in 1986, *Alias Grace* in 1996, and *Oryx and Crake* in 2003. Considered one of Canada's greatest writers, Atwood continues to write to critical acclaim: her recent publication *Madd-Addam* (2013) provides a "magnificent final instalment" (Adair, 2013: para. 3) to *The Madd-Addam Trilogy*. She repeatedly explores the politics of Canadian identity, environmental issues and, despite her discomfort with the 'feminist' label, women's rights. She writes within the realm of science fiction, dystopia, fantasy/myth and historical fiction.

THE HANDMAID'S TALE

A DYSTOPIAN NOVEL

- **Genre:** novel
- **Reference edition:** Atwood, M. (1996) *The Handmaid's Tale*. London: Vintage.
- **1st edition:** 1985
- **Themes:** politics, women's rights, sex, oppression and power, language, morality

The Handmaid's Tale (1986) is set in a future world called the Republic of Gilead, once the United States of America. Gilead was formed by a group of religious extremists called the 'Sons of Jacob', who replaced democracy with Christian theocracy. Under this totalitarian regime, the Sons of Jacob have severely repressed human rights and abolished women's rights entirely, reorganising society into Old Testament-inspired hierarchies. As most women in Gilead are infertile due to pollution, the government has created the Handmaids in an attempt to deal with the declining birth rate, where young women with healthy reproductive systems are forced to bear the children of high-ranking commanders. Focusing the story on one young Handmaid named Offred, Atwood lays bare the chillingly painful effects of authoritarian brutality.

SUMMARY

THE HELL OF GILEAD

The novel opens in a school gymnasium, where the narrator and other women are being imprisoned. The women are forbidden to speak with each other or walk freely outside the building, and are monitored by those the narrator calls 'Aunt Sara', 'Aunt Elizabeth' and 'Aunt Lydia': stripped of any autonomy, they have become "ladies in reduced circumstances" (p. 18). As we are to learn as the novel progresses, this is the Women's Centre. The story then jumps forward in time, where the narrator Offred is working as a Handmaid for a Commander married to Serena Joy, once a famous soprano singer. The narrator has been in this post for five weeks, and we learn that she has previously had two postings to different officials. Her job is to have sex with the Commander (a mechanical process named the Ceremony) in order to provide him and his Wife with a child. The Handmaids are permitted one walk a day, in pairs, around the Republic of

Gilead. Offred walks with a Handmaid called Ofglen. Atwood intersperses the narrator's present narrative with flashbacks and reflections. We jump back in time through the narrator's memories of her husband Luke, her daughter, her best friend Moira, her mother, and her life before the Republic's regime. We learn that Offred and Luke attempted to flee from Gilead across the Canadian boarder, but were captured and have since been separated.

BREAKING THE RULES ON THE INSIDE AND THE OUTSIDE

Atwood takes us through the narrator's walk with a Handmaid named Ofglen to "the thing [they've] in truth come to see: the Wall" (p. 41). The Wall is designed to trap people inside the Republic of Gilead, and is lined with the dead bodies of so-called war criminals. It is clear that under Gilead's oppressive regime, no individual can speak out against the state without fearing for their life: as such, the narrator "must not feel" and "won't give anything away" (p. 43). Offred then goes back to the Commander's home and, once dismissed, goes up to her room. She finds the Commander hovering outside her bedroom, "violating custom" (p. 59). Once the Commander hurries away, the narrator enters her bedroom and takes the reader through the space: we learn that the previous Handmaid left a message on the inside of the cupboard, "Nolite te bastardes carborundorum" (p. 62); however, Offred, and consequently perhaps the reader, does not yet know what this phrase means.

It is May. Atwood returns to Offred and Ofglen's walks, mirroring the earlier episode of the two looking at the wall. As they are leaving, Ofglen says "It's a beautiful May day" (p. 53). We later learn that the word 'Mayday' is the secret password of the resistance, the people working together against the Republic's oppressive regime; however, at this point in the novel it seems that the narrator does not fully understand the significance of Ofglen's choice of words.

In the night following one of the Ceremonies, the narrator illegally sneaks out of her room to steal something from Serena Joy's parlour. Surprisingly, she runs into Nick, the Commander's chauffeur, compromised in a similarly illegal act. He tells the narrator that he was coming to find her with a message that the Commander wants to see her tomorrow in his office. The Commander and Offred subsequently start meeting secretly. At first, they play Scrabble two to three nights a week. The Commander then begins buying the narrator gifts, such magazines and hand lotion, and in the meetings Offred is given the opportunity to read. On one occasion, Offred asks the Commander what the inscription on the inside of her cupboard means, and we learn that it translates to "don't let the bastards grind you down" (p. 197). We also learn that the previous Handmaid hanged herself. The narrator finds that their secret meetings make the Ceremonies more awkward, for "he was no longer a thing" (p. 170).

INCREASING RECKLESSNESS

Ofglen and Offred slowly grow closer. Through one brief exchange around halfway through the novel, the women come to the mutual understanding that neither of them are true believers in the Republic's cause. Ofglen and Offred start attending events together, for example Janine's childbirth and a Prayvaganza (weddings for the

Wives' daughters). A crucial event is when the two go to a Women's Salvaging, a public group execution at which women are forced to be present. A man is being put on trial for rape. During the trial, Ofglen surges forward and kicks the man in the head, knocking him out. Returning to Offred, she hastily explains that the man was not a rapist but "one of ours" (p. 292), on side of the resistance, and that she attacked him to put him out of his misery.

As the Commander has not yet managed to get Offred pregnant, Serena Joy privately requests that Offred secretly have sex with Nick. She schedules this for the same night that the Commander decides to take Offred out to a brothel called Jezebel's, with the intention of having sex with her outside of their usual Ceremonies. Whilst at the brothel, Offred sees her best friend Moira. We learn that Moira escaped the Women's Centre by impersonating an officer, dressed in brown uniform. For eight to nine months, she lived underground, moving slowly across the continent towards the border; however, she was captured in Salem. Rather than going back to the Women's Centre, Moira had to choose between going to the Colonies or working at Jezebel's, and picked the latter. Moira and Offred's reunion is emotional and raw. Parting with Moira, the Commander then takes Offred to a former hotel room to have sex, where Offred forces herself to fake enjoyment. Once they return to the house, Offred is ordered by Serena Joy to go and see Nick, and they have sex. However, after having slept with him on Serena's orders, Offred then begins to do so of her own accord. They develop feelings for each other, and she starts telling him secrets about her past and present. Offred soon suspects she may be pregnant.

OFFRED'S FATE

After the Women's Salvaging, Offred does not see Ofglen again, but is still permitted to resume her regular walks. Partnered with "the new Ofglen" (p. 295), Offred tries out the coded language of the resistance by dropping the phrase "May Day" (p. 296) into conversation. It is quickly apparent that the new Ofglen is a true believer in the Republic's movement, but is very aware of the resistance's codes; as such, she susses Offred out instantly. As a warning to Offred, the new Ofglen then tells her that the old Ofglen committed suicide, having been discovered as a member of the resistance. Returning home, Offred finds that Serena Joy has become aware of her secret arrangement with the Commander. Offred contemplates suicide. A black van comes for her seemingly sealing her fate; however, Nick arrives and tells Offred that they are members of the resistance coming to rescue her. As it is unclear whether Nick is being truthful, the novel's ending is ambiguous, and Offred's fate is as much confined to "the darkness within" as it is "the light" (p. 307).

After the narrative has ended, the book closes with a section titled 'Historical Notes', where Professor Pieixoto discusses the novel in 2195, after the fall of Gilead. The professor reveals that the narrator recorded her narrative on tapes that he then transcribed. Despite his research, the professor says that Offred's fate remains unclear.

CHARACTER STUDY

OFFRED

Offred is the narrator of the story and the novel's protagonist. However, her real name is not actually Offred. She "has another name, which no-body uses now because it's forbidden" (p. 94). Stripped of her own name and by consequence her previous self, her existence as 'Offred' is one she must fabricate in order to suit the Gilead regime:

> "My self is a thing I must now compose, as one composes a speech. What I must present is a made thing, not something born." (p. 76)

As such, Atwood asks the reader to distinguish between the performative Offred and the real, private self of the narrator. The former is obedient, quiet and submissive, and espouses the indoctrination of the Republic mechanically and unemotionally. As such, Offred can be interpreted as a passive figure who relies upon the more radical actions of the people around her. For example, if we are to believe that Nick is a member of the resistance, then Offred's 'escape' at the end of the novel is facilitated by the people around her. As H. S. Macpherson explains, Offred therefore becomes a "passive everywoman, awaiting rescue" (2010: 56).

However, whilst Offred is not as rebellious as Moira or Ofglen, she nonetheless holds onto her sense of autonomy in the subtlest of ways, for example by stealing things from the Commander's Wife, or making forbidden eye contact with a Guardian when out walking. Towards the latter half of the novel, the narrator's rebelliousness begins to dominate and crush the Offred that acts as a performative pawn of the Republic. In order to continue her forbidden relationship with Nick, for example, she "became reckless" and "took stupid chances" (p. 280). Similarly, although Offred rationally knows that she should "give it a week, two weeks, maybe longer" to gauge whether the new Ofglen is part of the resistance or not, she cannot bring herself to hold back (p. 296). Ultimately, her increasing recklessness throughout the novel demonstrates how her independence cannot be fully foiled or suppressed through indoctrination under the repressive regime.

Through the narrator's frequent flashbacks, the reader can piece together parts of her previous life. We learn that her relationship with Luke started as an affair, as Luke was previously married to another woman. We also learn that she tried to escape with Luke and their daughter, but they were captured at the border last minute. Under the Republic's regime, divorces were invalidated, making Offred an adulteress and therefore a sinner. As such, the Republic claimed the right to take away their child and give her to a 'legitimate' family, whilst Offred was forced to become a Handmaid. As Offred doubts that she will see any of her family again, her flashbacks are a painful articulation of grief. Offred flits between thinking of her daughter as "the ghost of a dead girl, the little girl who died when she was five" and maintaining some painful hope that she "still does exist" (p. 74). Offred is engaged in a similar mental battle when thinking of Luke: "Luke wasn't a doctor. Isn't" (p. 43). This change of tense from the past to the present demonstrates how she inadvertently slips into thinking about Luke as if he were dead, and has to correct herself into thinking of him as alive. The narrator's flashbacks to her family are therefore a clear illustration of the pain and grief that Offred continues to endure, but also a testament to her strength of will in maintaining hope that they may be out there somewhere.

THE COMMANDER

The relationship between Offred and the Commander is signified by the name 'Offred', which means 'Of Fred'. This implies that Offred directly belongs to the Commander as a piece of property to be used; as such, he represents the oppressive power structures to which Offred is subjected. However, as Atwood develops the secret meetings between Offred and the Commander, it becomes clear that he lives a sad existence, and is nostalgic for the time before the Republic's regime. This is demonstrated when Offred questions his motives for showing her an illegal magazine, expecting "that he was amusing himself, at [her] expense" (p. 166). However, the reality is that he simply craves companionship: "Who else could I show it to? He said, and there it was again, that sadness" (*ibid.*) Furthermore, the Commander admits that he and his Wife "don't seem to have much in common, these days" (*ibid.*) and it consequently becomes clear to both Offred and the reader that it is his loneliness that drives him to arrange their secret meetings.

Although Atwood evokes a degree of pity for the Commander, it is also apparent that he acts very selfishly. By feeding his desire for companionship, the Commander does not seem to even understand the extent to which he puts Offred's life at risk. For example, when the Commander gives her the hand lotion, he is ignorant of the fact that Offred cannot keep it in her own room in case it is found. And as Offred articulates, "it wasn't the first time he gave evidence of being truly ignorant of the real conditions under which we lived" (p. 167). As such, the Commander seems selfishly and naively blind to the effects of his actions. Similarly, by taking Offred to Jezebel's, the Commander intends to sleep with her outside their "impersonal" (p. 171) Ceremonies, with the hope that she "might enjoy it for a change" (p. 266): as such, the Commander puts Offred at risk in order to improve his sex life. Furthermore, the fact that the Commander even thinks it might be possible for Offred to "be, with him, any different" (p. 267) demonstrates how ignorant he is of the awfulness of her position as a Handmaid.

SERENA JOY

Serena Joy (the Commander's Wife), is a very unhappy, and by consequence spiteful, woman. Offred's frequent reflections on whether their situation is worse for her or Serena Joy are a testament to the fact that she is living a very troubled existence. However, any sympathy for Serena Joy is crushed by the way she treats Offred. Like the Commander, she too puts Offred in great risk by asking her to have sex with Nick in order to get pregnant, without any concern for Offred's fate. Moreover, in order to get her to agree to this scheme, Serena Joy offers to show Offred a picture of her daughter who she has not seen for three years; consequently, she emotionally manipulates Offred for her own personal gain. Likewise, when Serena Joy finds out about the affair between Offred and the Commander, she takes all her frustration out on Offred, despite the fact that she was completely passive in the arrangement.

Unlike Offred and Ofglen, Atwood offers a more detailed description of Serena Joy's appearance. She is described as having blonde hair, showing "from under her veil", with eyebrows "plucked into thin arched lines" and eyes of "flat hostile blue [...] a blue that shuts you out" (p. 25). By contrast, all we know of Offred's appearance is that she has "brown hair" and "stand[s] five seven without shoes" (p. 153), and of Ofglen only that her eyes are "brown" and that she is a "little plumper than [Offred]" (p. 29). Moreover, the fact that Offred and Ofglen are even described similarly reflects their lack of individuality under the Republic's oppressive regime. Setting the Handmaids' nondescript appearances against a much more detailed description of Serena Joy serves to exemplify this further.

MOIRA

Moira is Offred's best friend, and the only person from Offred's previous life who we get to meet. In Offred's flashbacks, Atwood depicts Moira as an incredibly strong-willed individual with a powerful sense of right and wrong. She is a character who fights for her freedom whatever the cost, and therefore becomes a figure of admiration and hope for Offred. However, when Offred finds her at Jezebel's, Moira's fighting spirit seems crushed by the totalitarian state. As Offred outlines:

> "I don't want her to be like me. Give in, go along, save her skin. That is what it comes down to. I want gallantry from her, swashbuckling, heroism, single-handed combat. Something I lack." (p. 261)

Moira's forced submission to life at Jezebel's also signifies Offred's loss of hope in the rebel cause, reflecting the extent to which the Republic of Gilead imposes tyrannical control. As their meeting at Jezebel's is the last time Offred sees Moira, neither the narrator nor the reader find out what happened to her.

ANALYSIS

NARRATIVE STRUCTURE

Atwood uses first person narration in *The Handmaid's Tale*, which means that Offred addresses the story directly to the reader. Offred herself acknowledges this, noting that "A story is like a letter. *Dear You*, I'll say. Just *you*, without a name" (p. 49), which evidences her authorial self-awareness. By positing herself as the author, Offred also constructs her reader:

> "By telling you anything at all I'm at least believing in you, I believe you're there, I believe you into being. Because I'm telling you this story I will your existence. I tell, therefore you are." (p. 279)

The final sentence of this section – "I tell, therefore you are" – is a play upon René Descartes' oft-quoted "I think, therefore I am". Yet by shifting the focus from "I" to "you", Atwood makes it clear that Offred wills her own idea of a reader into existence in a bid for her story to be heard. Consequently, this means that the events of the novel are filtered through Offred's eyes, and the reader can only witness events that Offred herself has access to. For example, because Offred does not witness what actually happens to the old Ofglen, the reader is similarly not permitted to find out. As such, both the reader and Offred can only take the new Ofglen's word for what happened, and as Offred acknowledges, it was "odd" for her to share this information with Offred (p. 297). Our knowledge of Moira's fate is similarly limited. The reader is denied knowledge of "how [Moira] ended" because of the fact that Offred "never saw her again" after their meeting at Jezebel's (p. 262). As Atwood's use of a first person narrative voice leaves the reader with narrative gaps, she therefore asks us to use our imagination and contemplate the possible scenarios that we are, by the nature of the narrative, denied.

Atwood also uses Offred's narrative voice to suggest that her version of events is only a reconstruction of the truth, as is evidenced through her re-telling of Moira's story. Offred acknowledges that she "can't remember exactly" what Moira said, but she both "filled it out for her" (p. 255) and "tried to make it sound as much like her" as possible (p. 256). Atwood consequently makes it clear that Offred's account of Moira's story is a version of the truth, asking us to ponder what may have been missed out or embellished. Atwood further undermines the reliability of Offred's narrative by having Offred change her own versions of events. For example, when telling the reader about her first night with Nick, Offred offers the reader two versions of events before settling on the fact that she is "not sure how it happened; not exactly" (p. 275). Continuing, "all I can hope for is a reconstruction: the way love feels is always approximate" (*ibid.*). Offred implies that certain moments or feelings cannot be put into words and instead exist beyond the limits of language. Consequently, Atwood uses this moment to suggest that Offred's words cannot quite capture the reality of her story.

Finally, Atwood's use of first person narration involves a series of flashbacks to Offred's life before the Republic of Gilead. The reader consequently pieces bits of information together as Offred relives them. Consequently, whilst a man named Luke is mentioned near the beginning of the novel (p. 43), it is not until later that we find out exactly who he is. Atwood therefore holds back on giving the reader Offred's full story in order to flesh out her individuality slowly, thus heightening the reader's intrigue. There is a sense that we grow to understand Offred gradually, and on her own terms.

IS THERE ANY HOPE FOR WOMEN?

In the Republic of Gilead all the women, including both the Handmaids and the Commanders' Wives, are judged on their ability (or inability) to conceive a child. Stripped of any sense of autonomy, the Handmaids are not allowed to socialise, read, or even set foot outside alone. The defining feature of Offred and the other handmaids is the fact that they have "viable ovaries" (p. 153) and are expected to have mechanical, emotionless sex with their Commanders. The Handmaids are thus thought of as machine-like vessels, designed to conceive a child and then give the baby up. This demonstrates how, in the Republic of Gilead, the Handmaids are "containers, it's only the insides of our bodies that are important" (p. 107). Offred's act of moisturising

her body with butter, and her subsequent re-
quest for hand lotion from the Commander, can
therefore be read as a means of preserving her
body's humanity:

> "As long as we do this, butter our skin to keep it
> soft, we can believe that we will some day get
> out, that we will be touched again, in love or
> desire." (*ibid.*)

The butter here becomes Offred's way of preserving hope that some day, she will be thought of as
more than just a container, and therefore reflects
her refusal to succumb to the body dysmorphia
instilled by the Republic's regime. Furthermore,
if the Handmaids have not conceived after three
postings to different Commanders, their existence is deemed worthless, and they are shipped
off to the Colonies.

It is difficult to argue that Atwood offers much
hope for women within the novel: the Handmaids
are trapped in an unbearable situation, and
Offred's best friend Moira – who is seen as an
independent fighter – is finally crushed within
the Republic of Gilead's regime. Furthermore,
Atwood shapes the Handmaids' reality into a

hellish, and therefore inescapable, existence, as is evidenced through one of Offred's psychological musings: "I [...] step sideways out of my own time. Out of time. Though this is time, nor am I out of it" (p. 47). Atwood's use of the phrase "though this is time, nor am I out of it" is an intertextual illusion to Christopher Marlowe's (English poet and playwright, 1564-1593) *Doctor Faustus*, wherein the devil Mephistopheles depicts hell as an endless psychological torture, saying "why this is hell, nor am I out of it". By alluding to Mephistopheles' discussion of hell, Atwood thereby suggests that Offred's "time" in Gilead is a hellish form of endless, inescapable entrapment. However, by reminding us of the unreliability of Offred's narration, Atwood simultaneously offers glimmers of hope. Considering her use of very ambiguous narrative endings, we do not find out precisely what happens to Moira, Offred or Ofglen. This in turn suggests an open-ended narrative tale that defies a single interpretation; Atwood therefore uses these ambiguous endings as a means of suggesting their hopeful escape from the bleak reality of Gilead. Meanwhile, Atwood's second futuristic narrative in the final section titled 'Historical Notes' confirms that the Republic of Gilead does indeed fall. However, whilst the reader is made aware of how the broad narrative of Gilead ends, we are still left wondering how Offred's individual narrative concludes:

> "As all historians know, the past is a great darkness, filled with echoes. Voices may reach us from it; but what they say to us is imbued with the obscurity of the matrix out of which they come" (p. 324)

The Professor's research then, is an attempt to piece together the "matrix" of history and understand its "obscurity", and Offred's narrative is an example of one of the voices that "may reach us". However, as the Professor admits that Offred's story "slips from our grasp and flees" (*ibid.*) the fate of these women remains very obscure.

GENERIC FUSION

As *The Handmaid's Tale* is set in an alternative world, it would not be unreasonable to suggest that the novel presents characteristics of the genre of science fiction. However, it is important to note that Atwood herself rejects this label in favour of 'speculative fiction'. In an article for *The Guardian* in 2005, Atwood writes that "the science fiction label belongs on books with things in them that we can't do yet, such as going through a wormhole in space to another universe"; however, speculative fiction "takes place on Planet Earth" and "employs the means already to hand" (2005: para. 2). Atwood's preference for 'speculative fiction' therefore demonstrates how she seeks to ground *The Handmaid's Tale* in reality, rather than removing it from "Planet Earth" (*ibid.*).

Atwood's 'speculative fiction' consequently draws on elements of dystopian literature, as *The Handmaid's Tale* is set in the near future United States and is designed to function as a warning for contemporary society. By focusing on women's rights (or lack thereof), *The Handmaid's Tale* becomes a social and political dystopia, responding critically to the political and religious conservatism of 1980s America and the history of American Puritanism. As Atwood imagines a seemingly unthinkable, exaggerated version of society, she grounds it in contemporary thinking, warning her readers what things could be like if the situation were to escalate. Furthermore, through Atwood's first person narrative structure, she focuses on one individual's experience of this dystopian world: as the reader witnesses the state's impact on a microscopic level, the story therefore becomes much more personal. In short, *The Handmaid's Tale* can be characterised as a piece of speculative fiction that uses a localised dystopian narrative in order to stress the importance of individual victims against totalitarian state power.

FURTHER REFLECTION

SOME QUESTIONS TO THINK ABOUT...

- Why do you think Atwood included the section 'Historical Notes' at the end of the novel?
- The *Houston Chronicle* described the book as "an excellent novel about the directions our lives are taking...Read it while it's still allowed." What are the implications of this description and to what extent do you agree?
- Comment on the way in which Atwood merges a dystopian setting with a depiction of old-fashioned Christian theocratic rule.
- What effect does Atwood create by addressing the reader directly, through Offred's narrative voice?
- Over the last 30 years, *The Handmaid's Tale* has been banned and challenged in numerous schools. Why do you think this is?
- What do you think happened to Moira, Offred, Luke and Offred's daughter?
- Is Nick trustworthy? Justify your answer.

- *The Handmaid's Tale* has often been compared to George Orwell's *1984*. How are these novels similar and different?
- Discuss the theme of power within the novel.
- *The Handmaid's Tale* has recently been adapted into a TV series. In what ways is the novel still relevant in today's society?
- How does Atwood portray the passing of time?

We want to hear from you!
Leave a comment on your online library
and share your favourite books on social media!

FURTHER READING

REFERENCE EDITION

- Atwood, M. (1996) *The Handmaid's Tale*. London: Vintage.

REFERENCE STUDIES

- Adair, T. (2013) Book Review: Madd-Addam by Margaret Atwood. *The Scotsman*. [Online]. [Accessed 20 September 2018]. Available from: <https://www.scotsman.com/lifestyle/culture/books/book-review-madd-addam-by-margaret-attwood-1-3061728>

- Atwood, M. (2005) Aliens have taken the place of angels. *The Guardian*. [Online] [Accessed 20 September 2018]. Available from: <https://www.theguardian.com/film/2005/jun/17/sciencefiction-fantasyandhorror.margaretatwood>

- Macpherson, H. S. (2010) *The Cambridge Introduction to Margaret Atwood*. Cambridge: Cambridge University Press.

ADDITIONAL SOURCES

- Cooke, N. (2004) *Margaret Atwood: A Critical Companion*. London: Greenwood Press.

- Cooke, N. (1998) *Margaret Atwood: A Biography*. Toronto: ECW Press.

- Howells, C. A. (2006) *The Cambridge Companion to Margaret Atwood*. Cambridge: Cambridge University Press.

ADAPTATIONS

- *The Handmaid's Tale*. (2017-present) [TV Series]. Bruce Miller. Dir. Canada: Daniel Wilson Productions Inc., The Littlefield Company, White Oak Pictures, MGM Television.

- *The Handmaid's Tale*. (1990) [Film]. Volker Schlöndorff. Dir. USA/Germany: Biskop Film, Cinecom Entertainment Group, Cinétudes Films, Daniel Wilson Productions Inc., Master Partners, Odyssey.

Although the editor makes every effort to
verify the accuracy of the information published,
BrightSummaries.com accepts no responsibility for
the content of this book.

www.brightsummaries.com

Ebook EAN: 9782808012676

Paperback EAN: 9782808012683

Legal Deposit: D/2018/12603/389

Cover: © Primento

Digital conception by Primento, the digital partner of
publishers.

Made in the USA
Coppell, TX
14 August 2021